SLAVES IN ALGIERS

SLAVES IN ALGIERS; OR, A STRUGGLE FOR FREEDOM: A PLAY, INTERSPERSED WITH SONGS, IN THREE ACTS

Susanna Haswell Rowson

a *Broadview Anthology of American Literature* edition

Contributing Editor, *Slaves in Algiers*: Nora Ruddock

General Editors, *The Broadview Anthology of American Literature*:

Derrick R. Spires, Cornell University
Rachel Greenwald Smith, Saint Louis University
Christina Roberts, Seattle University
Joseph Rezek, Boston University
Justine S. Murison, University of Illinois, Urbana-Champaign
Laura L. Mielke, University of Kansas
Christopher Looby, University of California, Los Angeles
Rodrigo Lazo, University of California, Irvine
Alisha Knight, Washington College
Hsuan L. Hsu, University of California, Davis
Michael Everton, Simon Fraser University
Christine Bold, University of Guelph

broadview press

BROADVIEW PRESS – www.broadviewpress.com
Peterborough, Ontario, Canada

Founded in 1985, Broadview Press remains a wholly independent publishing house. Broadview's focus is on academic publishing: our titles are accessible to university and college students as well as scholars and general readers. With over 800 titles in print, Broadview has become a leading international publisher in the humanities, with world-wide distribution. Broadview is committed to environmentally responsible publishing and fair business practices.

Library and Archives Canada Cataloguing in Publication

Title: Slaves in Algiers, or, A struggle for freedom : a play, interspersed with songs, in three acts / Susanna Haswell Rowson; contributing editor, Nora Ruddock.
Other titles: Struggle for freedom
Names: Rowson, Mrs., 1762-1824, author. | Ruddock, Nora, 1978- editor.
Description: Broadview anthology of American literature edition | Series statement: Broadview Anthology of American Literature | Includes bibliographical references.
Identifiers: Canadiana (print) 20230175864 | Canadiana (ebook) 20230175953 | ISBN 9781554816354 (softcover) | ISBN 9781770489059 (PDF) | ISBN 9781460408377 (EPUB)
Classification: LCC PS2736.R3 S53 2023 | DDC 813/.2—dc23

Broadview Press handles its own distribution in North America:
PO Box 1243, Peterborough, Ontario K9J 7H5, Canada
555 Riverwalk Parkway, Tonawanda, NY 14150, USA
Tel: (705) 743-8990; Fax: (705) 743-8353
email: customerservice@broadviewpress.com

For all territories outside of North America, distribution is handled by Eurospan Group.

Broadview Press acknowledges the financial support of the Government of Canada for our publishing activities.

Canada

Developmental Editor: Nora Ruddock
Cover Designer: Lisa Brawn
Typesetter: Alexandria Stuart

PRINTED IN CANADA

Contents

Introduction • 7

    Susanna Haswell Rowson • 7

    Slaves in Algiers; or, A Struggle for Freedom: A Play,
      Interspersed with Songs, in Three Acts • 10

Slaves in Algiers; or, A Struggle for Freedom: A Play,
Interspersed with Songs, in Three Acts • 15

Introduction

Susanna Haswell Rowson
c. 1762 – 1824

Susanna Rowson was the author of America's first best-selling sentimental romance, *Charlotte Temple*, but her prolific transatlantic career spanned many genres and roles. In addition to influencing the history of the American novel with her prose fiction, she was a well-known actor and playwright, and, later in life, she founded a successful school for girls and became a respected educator. An early professional writer who judiciously crafted her own celebrity, she described herself as an "Englishwoman" but wrote about the new nation of America with fierce patriotism—and with particular attention to the trials and virtues of American womanhood. Though she approached this last subject with varying degrees of radicalism and conservatism during her long career, her novels and plays consistently explore feminist themes. This made her a controversial figure, derided as "the American Sappho" but also praised for "elevat[ing] the moral character of her own sex."

Rowson was born Susanna Haswell in Portsmouth, England, into an educated, military family. Her father was a naval officer; her mother died of complications from childbirth when Susanna was ten days old. Rowson spent a happy childhood in Massachusetts, where her father was stationed, and she was educated at home. She became well-read in contemporary literature and philosophy, aided in part by her family's friendship with the activist James Otis (1725–83), who took an interest in her education and was an early influence. Famous for coining the phrase "Taxation without

Representation is tyranny," Otis was an advocate of colonial rights and of African American rights, and his dedication to Enlightenment ideals of freedom and equality had a deep and lasting effect on Rowson.

The Revolutionary War changed things for Rowson's loyalist family, as they were interned in 1775. The family was then freed by means of a prisoner exchange, and they returned to England in 1778. Much later, in a defense of her own patriotism, she would describe herself as "equally attached to either country":

> the unhappy dissentions affected me in the same manner as a person may be imagined to feel, who having a tender lover, and an affectionate brother who are equally dear to her heart, and by whom she is equally beloved, sees them engaged in a quarrel with, and fighting against each other, when, let whichsoever party conquer, she cannot be supposed insensible to the fate of the vanquished.

The family's property in America was confiscated, and they lived in England in straitened circumstances, selling Rowson's inheritance to support themselves. She also took a position as governess to contribute to the family income.

Rowson began her writing career in 1786, publishing *Victoria. A Novel in Two Volumes*. In the same year she married William Rowson, a struggling businessperson with a passion for the theater. He was supportive of Susanna's writing—in part because the couple needed the money she earned—and shortly after her marriage Susanna became increasingly involved in the theater herself, publishing an anonymous satirical critique of the London scene, *A Trip to Parnassus* (1788). She also continued to produce novels, including *The Inquisitor; or, Invisible Rambler* (1788), a series of vignettes inspired by Laurence Sterne's *A Sentimental Journey* (1768). A moralistic romance, *Mary, or the Test of Honour*, followed in 1789, and in 1791 she published *Mentoria*, a collection of dialogues and tales, as well as the sentimental novel *Charlotte Temple* (under the title *Charlotte. A Tale of Truth*).

Charlotte Temple was a modest success in England, but its sales were not substantial enough to offset the failure of William Rowson's hardware business, and the couple moved to Edinburgh to join a theater company in 1791. They did well as actors, and in 1793 they traveled to Philadelphia to join the New Theater Company. In America, Susanna kept up an intense working life, acting at night and writing by day. On 30 June 1794, she premiered her first full-length comic opera, *Slaves in Algiers; or, A Struggle for Freedom*. Like many of Rowson's later plays, *Slaves in Algiers* focuses on its female characters and expresses a conservative feminism strongly influenced by Mary Wollstonecraft's *A Vindication of the Rights of Woman*, which had been published in Philadelphia in 1792. The often-quoted couplet from the epilogue of *Slaves in Algiers*—"Women were born for universal sway; / Men to adore, be silent, and obey"—is likely intended somewhat ironically, but it does reflect the expansion of social and economic opportunities for American women in the Revolutionary period.

In 1794, Rowson arranged to have *Charlotte Temple* published in the United States. A cautionary tale of a young Englishwoman seduced and brought to New York, abandoned by her seducer, and left to die in childbirth, the novel became a sensation and would be issued in over 225 editions, staying in print through to the end of the nineteenth century. Its popularity inaugurated a significant trend in sentimental fiction—and in novels by women—on the American literary scene. Now famous, Rowson continued to write plays at a fast pace, including *The Female Patriot. A Farce* (1794), *The Volunteers. A Farce* (1795), and *Americans in England. A Comedy* (1795). In the same span of years she released American editions of some of her earlier English books, as well as the new novel *Trials of the Human Heart* (1795). None of these approached the success of *Charlotte Temple*, though *Rebecca; or, The Fille de Chambre* (English edition 1792, American edition 1794) was her second-most popular work.

Rowson retired from the stage in 1797 and opened "Mrs. Rowson's Academy for Young Ladies" in Boston. As headmistress, she taught the daughters of upper-class New England families and wrote textbooks and histories, including *Rowson's Abridgement of Universal Geography* (1805) and *Youth's First Steps in Geography* (1811). During the decades she spent running the Academy, her commitment to gender equality diminished; in her 1804 poem "Rights of Woman," she declares that women should enjoy self-respect and freedom to run their households, but that they should not "interfere / With politics, divinity, or law." Yet she continued to assert women's potential to "attain the goal of perfection as well as the other sex" in arts and literature, and her 1822 textbook *Exercises in History* offers biographies of great women, including queens and other political leaders, presented as models for her students. While headmistress, she continued to write and publish novels, as well as poetry and periodical literature. She taught at her school until 1822 and died two years later.

Rowson's literary reputation rested for a long time on the success of *Charlotte Temple*, which was generally dismissed by modernist literary critics as a work of sentimental fiction. Mid-twentieth-century critic Leslie Fiedler, for example, called her a "third-rate sentimentalist," and assessments such as these sidelined her writing until the late twentieth century. Since then, as popular and sentimental novels have received more scholarly attention, *Charlotte Temple* has once again become a canonical text, with critics tracing the novel's influence to important later writers such as Rebecca Harding Davis and Harriet Beecher Stowe. More recent critics have also appreciated Rowson's larger body of work, particularly the plays and textbooks, and have highlighted her contributions to the early national culture of the United States. The complexity of her approach to issues such as slavery and women's rights makes her an illuminating voice in the Revolutionary-era debate concerning who should constitute the "people" of America.

Slaves in Algiers; or, A Struggle for Freedom: A Play, Interspersed with Songs, in Three Acts

When Susanna Rowson published *Slaves in Algiers* in 1794, she dedicated it to the "Citizens of the United States of North America" and stated that her chief aim was "to place the social virtues [of the United States] in the fairest point of view, and hold up, to merited contempt and ridicule, their opposite vices." Set in an Algerian harem, the play extols the Enlightenment ideals of liberty and equality and censures Algerian culture, which Rowson stereotypes as hierarchical, lawless, and tyrannical toward women and enslaved people.

With its fervent nationalism, the play capitalized on current events: the capture and enslavement of Americans on the coast of North Africa was an ongoing problem, and anxiety about it united

Americans. Following Independence, when American trade ships were no longer protected by the British Navy, "Barbary" pirates from Northern African states—what are now Algeria, Morocco, Libya, and Tunisia—intensified their attacks on American ships in the Mediterranean Sea, demanding tribute payments. If refused, they would pillage the ships and press Americans into slavery, holding them for ransom. The spectacle of white slavery and the high cost of tribute— by 1797 the U.S. government was giving a fifth of its annual budget to the Barbary states—incensed Americans and would in time lead to the establishment of the U.S. Navy. When Rowson wrote her play, public reaction to the ongoing piracy had reached a high pitch. Citizen groups were petitioning the government for action and holding fundraisers to pay ransoms, and dozens of narratives and plays were published on the subject.

While Rowson's depiction of Algiers suggests little knowledge of or interest in the real place or its people, *Slaves in Algiers* does reflect Rowson's extensive knowledge of British theater, and her portrayal of Islamic and Jewish characters especially draws upon stereotypes that were commonplace on the English stage in her era. In the character of Ben Hassan, for example, Rowson deploys the anti-Semitic trope of the deceitful, selfish Jewish moneylender, a character both villainized in other Barbary narratives and ridiculed in other stage comedies. Another stock type in the play is Muley Moloc, who embodies the trope of the cruelly repressive, sexually licentious Muslim tyrant. Even Muley Moloc's name is borrowed from theater history; variations on the name are attached to Islamic rulers in a variety of British plays, including John Dryden's *Don Sebastian* (1689), where the villain is the brutal "Muley-Moluch, Emperor of Barbary." Parallel plot elements and character relationships in *Don Sebastian* and *Slaves in Algiers* suggest that Dryden's play may have directly influenced Rowson's—as, it appears, did Aaron Hill's *Zara* (1735), a tragedy surrounding a Christian held captive by a tyrannical Muslim.

Rowson also follows several London playwrights—Isaac Bickerstaffe, Elizabeth Inchbald, and Hannah Cowley among them—by setting the action of her play in a harem, and by using this setting to depict women as enslaved to men, establishing an implicit link between gender equality and "civilized" (i.e., white) society. Yet, while a few years later Rowson would denounce the slave trade as "a disgrace to humanity," *Slaves in Algiers* does not explicitly draw the analogy—made by many other Barbary narratives—between white slavery in Africa and black slavery in America. *Slaves in Algiers* was written four years after the Naturalization Act designated only "free white persons" as "citizens" of America, and Rowson's characterization, plot, and nationalistic rhetoric does not challenge this narrow definition of who was to be accorded the rights of citizenship in the new republic.

The theater scene in Philadelphia in the late eighteenth century included a season of "benefits," individual performances in which ticket sales were given to lead actors. The premiere of *Slaves in Algiers* on 30 June 1794 was one such benefit performance, in which Susanna Rowson and her husband were assigned the profits. They both acted in the play, with Susanna taking the role of Olivia and delivering the epilogue as herself, while William performed a song between acts. The playbill in the *Philadelphia Gazette* also advertised "Mrs. Rowson" as the writer of the play, capitalizing on her fame as the author of the popular sentimental novel *Charlotte Temple* as a means to draw in a full house. A review in the *Gazette* praised Rowson's acting and moral rectitude, her "delicatesse and sound sense." The play enjoyed modest success in America, with performances in New York City and Baltimore, and was sufficiently popular to be released in print in the same year it was staged. It was also revived in Boston in 1816 after renewed American hostilities with the Barbary states spurred fresh interest in the subject matter. In recent decades, critics have given increased attention to *Slaves in Algiers*, explicating its interwoven feminist, nationalist, and imperialist themes, as well as its treatment of Muslim and Jewish characters.

Note on the Text

The text of the play is based on the 1794 edition, printed in Philadelphia by Wrigley and Berriman. Spelling and punctuation have been modernized in accordance with the practices of *The Broadview Anthology of American Literature*.

CR

SLAVES in ALGIERS;

OR, A

STRUGGLE for FREEDOM:

A PLAY,

INTERSPERSED WITH SONGS,

IN THREE ACTS.

By Mrs. ROWSON.

AS PERFORMED

AT THE

𝔑𝔢𝔴 𝔗𝔥𝔢𝔞𝔱𝔯𝔢𝔰,

IN

PHILADELPHIA and BALTIMORE.

PHILADELPHIA:

PRINTED FOR THE AUTHOR, BY WRIGLEY AND
BERRIMAN, N°. 149, CHESNUT-STREET.

M,DCC,XCIV.

Slaves in Algiers; or, A Struggle for Freedom: A Play, Interspersed with Songs, in Three Acts

To the Citizens of the United States of North America. This First Dramatic Effort Is Inscribed, By Their Obliged Friend, and Humble Servant, S. Rowson

PREFACE

In offering the following pages to the public, I feel myself necessitated to apologize for the errors which I am fearful will be evident to the severe eye of criticism.

The thought of writing a dramatic piece was hastily conceived, and as hastily executed; it being not more than two months, from the first starting of the idea, to the time of its being performed.

I feel myself extremely happy in having an opportunity thus publicly to acknowledge my obligation to Mr. Reinagle,[1] for the attention he manifested, and the taste and genius he displayed in the composition of the music. I must also return my thanks to the performers, who so readily accepted, and so ably supported their several characters: since it was chiefly owing to their exertions, that the play was received with such unbounded marks of approbation.

Since the first performance, I have made some alterations; and flatter myself those alterations have improved it: But of that, as well as of its merits in general, I am content to abide the decision of a candid and indulgent public.

Some part of the plot is taken from the story of the captive, related by Cervantes, in his inimitable romance of *Don Quixote*;[2] the rest is entirely the offspring of fancy.

---

1   *Mr. Reinagle*   Alexander Reinagle (1756–1809), American composer and musician. He was an important influence in the Philadelphia music and theater scene through the 1790s.

2   *story of the captive ... Don Quixote*   In chapters 40–41 of Miguel de Cervantes's *Don Quixote* (1605, 1615), a soldier tells Don Quixote about his captivity in Algiers and his subsequent escape. A young woman, Zoraida, gives him ransom money so he can free himself; Zoraida and the soldier escape to Spain, Zoraida converts to Christianity, and the two are married.

I am fully sensible of the many disadvantages under which I consequently labour from a confined education; nor do I expect my style will be thought equal in elegance or energy to the productions of those who, fortunately, from their sex, or situation in life, have been instructed in the classics, and have reaped both pleasure and improvement by studying the ancients in their original purity.

My chief aim has been to offer to the public a dramatic entertainment, which, while it might excite a smile, or call forth the tear of sensibility, might contain no one sentiment in the least prejudicial to the moral or political principles of the government under which I live.[1] On the contrary, it has been my endeavour, to place the social virtues in the fairest point of view, and hold up, to merited contempt and ridicule, their opposite vices. If, in this attempt, I have been the least successful, I shall reap the reward to which I aspire, in the smiles and approbation of a liberal public.

PROLOGUE

Written and Spoken by Mr. Fennel.[2]

When aged Priam, to Achilles' tent
To beg the captive corse° of Hector[3] went,   *corpse*
The silent suppliant spoke the father's fears,
His sighs his eloquence—his prayers his tears.
5 The noble conqueror by the sight was won,
And to the weeping sire restored the son.

No great Achilles holds *your* sons in chains,
No heart alive to friends' or father's pains,
No generous conqueror who is proud to show,
10 That valour vanquished is no more his foe;
But one, whose idol is his pilfered gold,

---

1 *government under which I live*   I.e., the American government.
2 *Mr. Fennel*   James Fennell (1766–1816), an English actor who was a star in the Philadelphia theater scene.
3 *Priam ... Hector*   In Book 24 of the *Iliad*, Priam, king of Troy, pleads with the Greek warrior Achilles, who has killed Priam's son Hector in battle and refused to return the body, instead mistreating it out of rage toward Hector.

Got, or° by piracy, or subjects sold.   *either*
Him no fond father's prayers nor tears can melt,
Untaught to feel for what he never felt.
What then behoves it, they who helped to gain,   15
A nation's freedom, feel the galling chain?
They, who a more than ten year's war[1] withstood,
And stamped their country's honour with their blood?
Or, shall the noble Eagle see her brood,
Beneath the pirate kite's° fell claw subdued?   *bird of prey*   20
View her dear sons of liberty enslaved,
Nor let them share the blessings which they saved?
It must not be—each heart, each soul must rise,
Each ear must listen to their distant cries;
Each hand must give, and the quick sail unfurled   25
Must bear their ransom to the distant world.

Nor *here* alone Columbia's° sons be free,   *America's*
Where'er they breathe there must be liberty.
There *must!* There *is*, for he who formed the whole,
Entwined blest freedom with th' immortal soul.   30
Eternal twins, whose mutual efforts fan,
That heavenly flame that gilds the life of man,
Whose light, 'midst manacles and dungeons drear,
The sons of honour, must forever cheer.

What tyrant then the virtuous heart can bind?   35
'Tis vices only can enslave the mind.
Who barters country, honour, faith, to save
His life, though free in person, is a slave.
While he, enchained, imprisoned though he be,
Who lifts his arm for liberty, is free.   40

Tonight, our author boldly dares to choose,
This glorious subject for her humble muse;
Though tyrants check the genius which they fear,
She dreads no check, nor persecution *here*;

---

1 *ten year's war* I.e., the American Revolutionary War (1775–83).

45 Where safe asylums every virtue guard,
And every talent meets its just reward.

Some say—the Comic muse, with watchful eye,
Should catch the reigning *vices* as they fly,
Our author boldly has reversed that plan,
50 The reigning virtues she has dared to scan,
And though a woman, plead the Rights of Man.
Thus she, with anxious hope her fate abides,
And to your care, the tender plant confides,
Convinced you'll cherish, what to freedom's true;
55 She trusts its life, to candour and to you.

DRAMATIS PERSONAE

MEN
Muley Moloc, Dey[1] of Algiers
Mustapha
Ben Hassan, a Renegado[2]
Sebastian, a Spanish Slave
Augustus, American Captive
Frederic, American Captive
Henry, American Captive
Constant, American Captive
Sadi
Selim

WOMEN
Zoriana, Moriscan[3] Woman
Fetnah, Moriscan Woman
Selima, Moriscan Woman
Rebecca, American Woman
Olivia, American Woman

Slaves.—Guards, etc.

---

1   *Dey*   Title of the absolute ruler of Algiers.
2   *Renegado*   Traitor or turncoat.
3   *Moriscan*   Moorish (term used to describe a person from North Africa).

(Apartment at the Dey's. [Enter] Fetnah and Selima.)

FETNAH.   Well, it's all vastly pretty, the gardens, the house and these
fine clothes, I like them very well, but I don't like to be confined.

SELIMA.   Yet, surely, you have no reason to complain; chosen favourite of the Dey, what can you wish for more.

FETNAH.   O, a great many things—in the first place, I wish for liberty.   5
Why do you talk of my being a favourite; is the poor bird that is
confined in a cage (because a favourite with its enslaver) consoled
for the loss of freedom? No! Though its prison is of golden wire,
its food delicious, and it is overwhelmed with caresses, its little
heart still pants for liberty: gladly would it seek the fields of air,   10
and even, perched upon a naked bough, exulting, carol forth its
song, nor once regret the splendid house of bondage.

SELIMA.   Ah! But then our master loves you.

FETNAH.   What of that, I don't love him.

SELIMA.   Not love him?   15

FETNAH.   No—he is old and ugly, then he wears such tremendous
whiskers; and when he makes love, he looks so grave and stately,
that I declare, if it was not for fear of his huge scimitar,[1] I should
burst out a-laughing in his face.

SELIMA.   Take care you don't provoke him too far.   20

FETNAH.   I don't care how I provoke him, if I can but make him
keep his distance. You know I was brought here only a few days
since—well, yesterday, as I was amusing myself, looking at the
fine things I saw everywhere about me, who should bolt into
the room, but that great, ugly thing, Mustapha. What do you   25
want, said I? Most beautiful Fetnah, said he, bowing till the tip
of his long, hooked nose almost touched the toe of his slipper—
most beautiful Fetnah, our powerful and gracious master, Muley
Moloc, sends me, the humblest of his slaves, to tell you, he will
condescend to sup in your apartment tonight, and commands   30
you to receive the high honour with proper humility.

SELIMA.   Well—and what answer did you return?

---

1   *scimitar*   Short, curved sword used primarily in the Middle East.

FETNAH.   Lord, I was so frightened, and so provoked, I hardly know
what I said, but finding the horrid looking creature didn't move,
35   at last I told him, that if the Dey was determined to come, I
supposed he must, for I could not hinder him.

SELIMA.   And did he come?

FETNAH.   No—but he made me go to him, and when I went trembling into the room, he twisted his whiskers and knit his great
40   beetle brows.[1] Fetnah, said he, you abuse my goodness, I have
condescended to request you to love me. And then he gave me
such a fierce look, as if he would say, and if you don't love me, I'll
cut your head off.

SELIMA.   I dare say you were finely frightened.

45 FETNAH.   Frightened! I was provoked beyond all patience, and
thinking he would certainly kill me one day or other, I thought I
might as well speak my mind, and be dispatched out of the way
at once.

SELIMA.   You make me tremble.

50 FETNAH.   So, mustering up as much courage as I could; great and
powerful Muley, said I—I am sensible I am your slave; you took
me from an humble state, placed me in this fine palace, and gave
me these rich clothes; you bought my person of my parents, who
loved gold better than they did their child; but my affections you
55   could not buy. I can't love you. How! cried he, starting from his
seat: how, can't love me? And he laid his hand upon his scimitar.

SELIMA.   Oh dear! Fetnah.

FETNAH.   When I saw the scimitar half drawn, I caught hold of his
arm. Oh! good my lord, said I, pray do not kill a poor little girl
60   like me; send me home again, and bestow your favour on some
other, who may think splendor a compensation for the loss of
liberty. Take her away, said he, she is beneath my anger.

SELIMA.   But, how is it Fetnah, that you have conceived such an
aversion to the manners of a country where you were born.

65 FETNAH.   You are mistaken. I was not born in Algiers. I drew my
first breath in England; my father, Ben Hassan, as he is now
called, was a Jew. I can scarcely remember our arrival here, and

---

1   *beetle brows* Heavy, dark eyebrows, associated with surliness.

have been educated in the Moorish religion,[1] though I always had a natural antipathy to their manners.

SELIMA. Perhaps imbibed from your mother. 70

FETNAH. No; she has no objection to any of their customs, except that of their having a great many wives at a time. But some few months since, my father, (who sends out many corsairs,[2]) brought home a female captive, to whom I became greatly attached; it was she who nourished in my mind the love of liberty, and taught me 75 woman was never formed to be the abject slave of man. Nature made us equal with them, and gave us the power to render ourselves superior.

SELIMA. Of what nation was she?

FETNAH. She came from that land, where virtue in either sex is the 80 only mark of superiority. She was an American.

SELIMA. Where is she now?

FETNAH. She is still at my father's, waiting the arrival of her ransom, for she is a woman of fortune. And though I can no longer listen to her instructions, her precepts are engraven on my heart. I feel that 85 I was born free, and while I have life, I will struggle to remain so.

SONG.

I.

The rose just bursting into bloom,
Admired where'er 'tis seen;
Diffuses round a rich perfume,
The garden's pride and queen. 90
When gathered from its native bed,
No longer charms the eye;
Its vivid tints are quickly fled,
'Twill wither, droop, and die.

II.

So woman when by nature dressed, 95
In charms devoid of art;

---

1 *Moorish religion* I.e., Islam.
2 *corsairs* Cruisers sent to pillage foreign ships and capture those on board.

Can warm the stoic's icy breast,
Can triumph o'er each heart.
Can bid the soul to virtue rise,
100   To glory prompt the brave,
But sinks oppressed, and drooping dies,
When once she's made a slave.

(*Exit.*)

ACT 1, SCENE 2

(*Ben Hassan's house. [Enter] Rebecca.*)

REBECCA.   (*Discovered reading.*) The soul, secure in its existence, smiles
At the drawn dagger, and defies its point.
The stars shall fade away, the sun itself
Grow dim with age, and nature sink in years,
5   But thou shall flourish in immortal youth,
Unhurt, amidst the war of elements,
The wreck of matter, or the crush of worlds.[1]

[*Puts down the book.*]

Oh! Blessed hope, I feel within myself that spark of intellectual heavenly fire, that bids me soar above this mortal world, and all
10   its pains or pleasures—its pleasures! Oh! Long—long since I have been dead to all that bear the name. In early youth, torn from the husband of my heart's election, the first only object of my love— bereft of friends, cast on an unfeeling world, with only one poor stay[2] on which to rest the hope of future joy. I have a son—my
15   child!—my dear Augustus—where are you now? In slavery. Grant

---

1   *The soul ... crush of worlds*   Rebecca is reading from *Cato* (1712), a play by Joseph Addison. See *Cato* 5.1.24–30. Cato the Younger (95–46 BCE) was a Roman political figure who died by suicide rather than accept the dictatorship of Julius Caesar. At this point in Addison's play, Cato is contemplating the immortality of his soul as he determines to kill himself rather than lose his freedom.

2   *stay*   Support.

me patience, Heaven! Must a boy born in Columbia,[1] claiming liberty as his birth-right, pass all his days in slavery? How often have I gazed upon his face, and fancied I could trace his father's features; how often have I listened to his voice, and thought his father's spirit spoke within him? Oh! My adored boy! Must I no more behold his eyes beaming with youthful ardour, when I have told him, how his brave countrymen purchased their freedom with their blood? Alas! I see him now but seldom; and when we meet, to think that we are slaves, poor, wretched slaves each serving different masters, my eyes overflow with tears. I have but time to press him to my heart, entreat just Heaven to protect his life, and at some future day restore his liberty.

(*Enter Ben Hassan.*)

BEN HASSAN. How do you do, Mrs. Rebecca?

REBECCA. Well, in health, Hassan, but depressed in spirit.

BEN HASSAN. Ah! Dat be very bad—come, come, cheer up, I vants to talk vid you, you must not be so melancholy, I be your very good friend.

REBECCA. Thank you, Hassan, but if you are in reality the friend you profess to be, leave me to indulge my grief in solitude. Your intention is kind, but I would rather be alone.

BEN HASSAN. You likes mightily to be by yourself, but I must talk to you a little; I vantsh to know ven you think your ransom vil come, 'tis a long time, Mrs. Rebecca, and you knows.

REBECCA. Oh yes, I know, I am under many obligations to you, but I shall soon be able to repay them.

BEN HASSAN. That may be, but 'tis a very long time, since you wrote to your friends, 'tis above eight months; I am afraid you have deceived me.

REBECCA. Alas! Perhaps I have deceived myself.

BEN HASSAN. Vat, den you have no friends—you are not a voman's of fortune?

REBECCA. Yes, yes, I have both friends and ability—but I am afraid my letters have miscarried.

---

1   *Columbia*   The United States, personified as Lady Liberty.

BEN HASSAN. Oh! dat ish very likely, you may be here dish two or
50 three years longer; perhaps all your lifetimes.

REBECCA. Alas! I am very wretched. (*Weeps.*)

BEN HASSAN. Come, now don't cry so; you must consider I never
suffered you to be exposed in the slave market.

REBECCA. But, my son. Oh! Hassan; why did you suffer them to
55 sell my child?

BEN HASSAN. I could not help it, I did all I could—but you knows I
would not let you be sent to the Dey, I have kept you in my own
house, at mine own expense. (*Aside.*) For which I have been more
than doubly paid.

60 REBECCA. That is indeed true, but I cannot at present return your
kindness.

BEN HASSAN. Ah! You be very sly rogue—you pretend not to know
how I loves you.

REBECCA. (*Aside.*) What means the wretch?

65 BEN HASSAN. You should forget your Christian friends, for I dare
say they have forgot you. I vill make you my vife, I vill give you
von, two, tree slaves to vait on you.

REBECCA. Make me your wife! Why, are you not already married?

BEN HASSAN. Ish, but our law gives us great many vives. Our law gives
70 liberty in love; you are an American, and you must love liberty.

REBECCA. Hold, Hassan; prostitute not the sacred word by apply-
ing it to licentiousness; the sons and daughters of liberty take
justice, truth, and mercy for their leaders when they list[1] under
her glorious banners.

75 BEN HASSAN. Your friends will never ransom you.

REBECCA. How readily does the sordid mind judge of others by
its own contracted feelings. You, who much I fear worship no
deity but gold, who could sacrifice friendship, nay, even the ties
of nature at the shrine of your idolatry, think other hearts as self-
80 ish as your own; but there are souls to whom the afflicted never
cry in vain, who, to dry the widow's tear, or free the captive,
would share their last possession. Blest spirits of philanthropy,
who inhabit my native land, never will I doubt your friendship,
for sure I am, you never will neglect the wretched.

---

1 *list* Enlist or enroll.

BEN HASSAN.   If you are not ransomed soon, I must send you to   85
the Dey.

REBECCA.   Even as you please. I cannot be more wretched than I am;
but of this be assured; however depressed in fortune, however
sunk in adversity, the soul secure in its own integrity will rise
superior to its enemies, and scorn the venal wretch who barters   90
truth for gold.

(*Exit [Rebecca].*)

BEN HASSAN.   (*Solus.*[1]) 'Tis a very strange voman, very strange
indeed; she does not know I got her pocket-book, with bills of
exchange in it; she thinks I keep her in my house out of charity,
and yet she talks about freedom and superiority, as if she was in   95
her own country. 'Tis devilish hard indeed, when masters may
not do what they please with their slaves. Her ransom arrived yesterday, but den she don't know it. Yesh, here is the letter; ransom
for Rebecca Constant, and six other Christian slaves; vell I vill
make her write for more, she is my slave, I must get all I can by   100
her. Oh, here comes that wild young Christian, Frederic, who
ransomed himself a few days since.

(*Enter Frederic.*)

FREDERIC.   Well, my little Israelite, what are you muttering about;
have you thought on my proposals, will you purchase the vessel
and assist us?   105

BEN HASSAN.   Vat did you say you would give me?

FREDERIC.   We can amongst us muster up two thousand sequins,[2]
'tis all we have in the world.

BEN HASSAN.   You are sure you can get no more?

FREDERIC.   Not a farthing more.   110

BEN HASSAN.   Den I vill be satisfied with dat, it will in some mea-
sure reward me—(*Aside.*) for betraying you.

FREDERIC.   And you will purchase the vessel.

---

1   *Solus*   Latin: Alone.
2   *sequins*   Gold coins.

BEN HASSAN.   I will do everything that is necessary—(*Aside.*) for my
own interest.

FREDERIC.   You have conveyed provision to the cavern by the sea
side, where I am to conceal the captives to wait the arrival of the
vessel.

BEN HASSAN.   Most shartingly,[1] I have provided for them as—
(*Aside.*) as secure a prison as any in Algiers.

FREDERIC.   But, are you not a most extortionate old rogue to require
so much, before you will assist a parcel of poor devils to obtain
their liberty?

BEN HASSAN.   Oh! Mr. Frederic, if I vash not your very good friend,
I could not do it for so little; the Moors are such uncharitable
dogs, they never think they can get enough for their slaves, but
I have a vasht deal of compassion; I feels very mush for the poor
Christians; I should be very glad—(*Aside.*) to have a hundred or
two of them my prisoners.

FREDERIC.   You would be glad to serve us?

BEN HASSAN.   Shartingly. (*Aside.*) Ven I can serve myself at the same
time.

FREDERIC.   Prithee, honest Hassan, how came you to put on the
turban?[2]

BEN HASSAN.   I'll tell you.

SONG.[3]

Ven I vas a mighty little boy,
Heart-cakes[4] I sold and pepper-mint drops;
Wafers and sweet chalk[5] I used for to cry,
Alacumpaine[6] and nice lolly-pops.

The next thing I sold vas the rollers for the macs[7]
To curl dere hair, 'twas very good;

---

1 *shartingly* Ben Hassan is likely combining "certainly" and "surely" here.
2 *put on the turban* I.e., become a Muslim.
3 *SONG* Rowson did not write this song; its authorship is unknown.
4 *Heart-cakes* Heart-shaped cakes.
5 *sweet chalk* Type of candy.
6 *Alacumpaine* Elecampane, otherwise known as horse-heal, a plant used as a tonic.
7 *rollers* Curling papers (for styling hair);   *macs* Macaronies, i.e., dandies.

Rosin I painted for[1] sealing wax
And I forged upon it vel brand en vast hood.[2]

Next to try my luck in the alley I vent,
But of dat I soon grew tired and wiser;   145
Monies I lent out at fifty per cent,
And my name was I.H. in the Public Advertiser.[3]

The next thing I did was a spirited prank,
Which at one stroke my fortune was made;
I wrote so very like the cashiers of the bank,   150
The clerks did not know the difference, and the monies was
    paid.

So, having cheated the Gentiles, as Moses commanded,[4]
Oh! I began to tremble at every gibbet°   *gallows*
    that I saw;
But I got on board a ship, and here was safely landed,
In spite of the judges, counsellors, attorneys, and law.   155

FREDERIC.   And so to complete the whole, you turned Mahometan.
BEN HASSAN.   Oh 'twas the safest way.
FREDERIC.   But Hassan, as you are so fond of cheating the Gentiles,
    perhaps you may cheat us.
BEN HASSAN.   Oh no! I swear by Mahomet.   160
FREDERIC.   No swearing, old Trimmer.[5] If you are true to us you will
    be amply rewarded, should you betray us, (*Sternly*.) by heaven

---

1   *for*   To look like.
2   *vel brand en vast hood*   Dutch: burn well and hold fast. This phrase, used to indicate
    the superior quality of Dutch sealing wax, was often dishonestly placed on poor-quality
    imitations.
3   *Public Advertiser*   London newspaper consisting primarily of advertisements.
4   *Gentiles*   Non-Jewish people;   *Moses commanded*   See Deuteronomy 23.19–20, where the
    Israelites are permitted to charge interest only when lending money to gentiles. This portion
    of Ben Hassan's song reflects a stereotypical association between Jews and moneylending.
    Moneylending was a common profession for Jewish people, as for hundreds of years social
    and legal discrimination in Europe prevented them from working in most professions,
    while religious doctrine forbade Christians from making loans for profit (a prohibition not
    always obeyed in practice).
5   *Trimmer*   One who changes sides out of self-interest.

165   you shall not live an hour after. Go, look for a vessel, make every
necessary preparation; and remember, instant death shall await
the least appearance of treachery.

BEN HASSAN.   But I have not got monies.

FREDERIC.   Go, you are a hypocrite; you are rich enough to purchase
an hundred vessels, and if the Dey knew of your wealth—

BEN HASSAN.   Oh! Dear Mr. Frederic, indeed I am very poor, but I
170   vill do all you desire, and you vill pay me afterwards. (*Aside.*) Oh,
I wish I could get you well paid with the bastinado.[1]

(*Exit.*)

FREDERIC.   (*Solus.*) I will trust this fellow no farther. I am afraid he
will play us false—but should he, we have yet one resource, we
can but die; and to die in a struggle for freedom, is better far than
175   to live in ignominious bondage.

(*Exit.*)

ACT 1, SCENE 3

(*Another Apartment at the Dey's. [Enter] Zoriana and Olivia.*)

ZORIANA.   Alas! It was pitiful, pray proceed.

OLIVIA.   My father's ill health obliging him to visit Lisbon, we
embarked for that place, leaving my betrothed lover to follow
us—but ere we reached our destined port, we were captured by
5   an Algerine corsair, and I was immediately sent to the Dey, your
father.

ZORIANA.   I was then in the country, but I was told he became
enamoured of you.

OLIVIA.   Unfortunately he did; but my being a Christian has hith-
10   erto preserved me from improper solicitations, though I am
frequently pressed to abjure my religion.

ZORIANA.   Were you not once near making your escape?

OLIVIA.   We were; my father, by means of some jewels which he had
concealed in his clothes, bribed one of the guards to procure false

---

1   *bastinado*   Stick used to torture people by striking them on the soles of the feet.

keys to the apartments, but on the very night when we meant to 15
put our plan in execution, the Dey, coming suddenly into the
room, surprized my father in my arms.

ZORIANA. Was not his anger dreadful?

OLIVIA. Past description. My dear father was torn from me and
loaded with chains, thrown into a dungeon where he still remains, 20
secluded from the cheering light of heaven; no resting place but
on the cold, damp ground; the daily portion of his food so poor
and scanty, it hardly serves to eke out an existence lingering as it
is forlorn.

ZORIANA. And where are the false keys? 25

OLIVIA. I have them still, for I was not known to possess them.

ZORIANA. Then banish all your sorrow; if you have still the keys,
tomorrow night shall set us all at liberty.

OLIVIA. Madam!

ZORIANA. Be not alarmed sweet Olivia, I am a Christian in my heart, 30
and I love a Christian slave, to whom I have conveyed money
and jewels, sufficient to ransom himself and several others. I will
appoint him to be in the garden this evening; you shall go with
me and speak to him.

OLIVIA. But how can we release my father? 35

ZORIANA. Every method shall be tried to gain admittance to his
prison; the Christian has many friends, and if all other means fail,
they can force the door.

OLIVIA. Oh! heavens, could I but see him once more at liberty, how
gladly would I sacrifice my own life to secure his. 40

ZORIANA. The keys you have will let us out of the house when all
are locked in the embraces of sleep; our Christian friends will be
ready to receive us, and before morning we shall be in a place of
safety. In the meantime, let hope support your sinking spirits.

SONG.

Sweet cherub clad in robes of white, 45
Descend celestial Hope;
And on thy pinions,° soft, and light, *wings*
Oh bear thy votary° up. *devotee*
'Tis thou can soothe the troubled breast,

The tear of sorrow dry;
Can'st lull each doubt and fear to rest,
And check the rising sigh.
Sweet cherub etc.

(*Exit.*)

ACT 1, SCENE 4

(*A garden—outside of a house, with small high lattices. [Enter] Henry and Frederic.*)

FREDERIC.   Fearing the old fellow would pocket our cash and betray us afterwards, I changed my plan, and have entrusted the money with a Spaniard, who will make the best bargain he can for us: have you tried our friends, will they be staunch?

5 HENRY.   To a man. The hope of liberty, like an electric spark, ran instantly through every heart, kindling a flame of patriotic ardour. Nay, even those whom interest or fear have hitherto kept silent, now openly avowed their hatred of the Dey and swore to assist our purpose.

10 FREDERIC.   Those whose freedom we have already purchased, have concerted proper measures for liberating many others, and by twelve o'clock tomorrow night, we shall have a party large enough to surround the palace of the Dey, and convey from thence in safety the fair Zoriana.

(*Window opens and a white handkerchief is waved.*)

15 HENRY.   Soft! Behold the signal of love and peace.
FREDERIC.   I'll catch it as it falls.

(*He approaches, it is drawn back.*)

HENRY.   'Tis not designed for you, stand aside.

(*Henry approaching; the handkerchief is let fall, a hand waved, and then the lattice shut.*)

'Tis a wealthy fall, and worth receiving.

FREDERIC. What says the fair Mahometan?

HENRY. Can I believe my eyes; here are English characters; and, but I think 'tis impossible, I should say, this was my Olivia's writing.

FREDERIC. This is always the way with you happy fellows, who are favourites with the women; you slight the willing fair one and dote on those who are only to be obtained with difficulty.

HENRY. I wish the lovely Moor had fixed her affections on you instead of me.

FREDERIC. I wish she had with all my soul—Moor or Christian, slave or free woman, 'tis no matter; if she was but young, and in love with me, I'd kneel down and worship her. But I'm a poor miserable dog; the women never say civil things to me.

HENRY. But, do you think it can be possible that my adorable Olivia is a captive here?

FREDERIC. Prithee man, don't stand musing and wondering, but remember this is the time for action. If chance has made your Olivia a captive, why, we must make a bold attempt to set her at liberty, and then I suppose you will turn over the fair Moriscan to me. But what says the letter.

HENRY. (*Reads.*) "As you have now the means of freedom in your power, be at the north garden gate at ten o'clock, and when you hear me sing, you will be sure all is safe, and that you may enter without danger; do not fail to come, I have some pleasant intelligence to communicate." Yes, I will go and acquaint her with the real state of my heart.

FREDERIC. And so make her our enemy.

HENRY. It would be barbarous to impose on her generous nature. What? Avail myself of her liberality to obtain my own freedom; take her from her country and friends, and then sacrifice her a victim to ingratitude and disappointed love?

FREDERIC. Tush, man, women's hearts are not so easily broken; we may, perhaps, give them a slight wound now and then, but they are seldom or never incurable.

HENRY. I see our master coming this way. Begone to our friends; encourage them to go through with our enterprise: the moment I am released I will join you.

FREDERIC.   'Till when, adieu.

(*Exit severally.*)

ACT 2, SCENE 1

(*Moonlight—A garden. [Enter] Zoriana and Olivia.*)

ZORIANA.   Sweet Olivia, chide me not; for though I'm fixed to leave this place and embrace Christianity, I cannot but weep when I think what my poor father will suffer. Methinks I should stay to console him for the loss of you.

5 OLIVIA.   He will soon forget me; has he not already a number of beautiful slaves, who have been purchased to banish me from his remembrance?

ZORIANA.   True, but he slights them all; you only are the mistress of his heart.

10 OLIVIA.   Hark, did you not hear a footstep?

ZORIANA.   Perhaps it is the young Christian; he waits the appointed signal. I think all is safe; he may approach.

SONG.

Wrapped in the evening's soft and pensive shade,
When passing zephyrs° scarce the   *breezes*
   herbage moves;
15 Here waits a trembling, fond, and anxious maid,
Expecting to behold the youth she loves.
Though Philomela[1] on a neighbouring tree,
Melodious warbles forth her nightly strain
Thy accents would be sweeter far to me,
20 Would from my bosom banish doubt and pain.
Then come dear youth, come haste away,
Haste to this silent grove,
The signal's given, you must obey,
'Tis liberty and love.

---

1 *Philomela* A nightingale. In Greek mythology, Philomela is transformed into a nightingale after she is raped by her brother-in-law Tereus, who ripped her tongue out so she could not denounce him.

(*Enter Henry.*)

HENRY.   Lovely and benevolent lady, permit me thus humbly to   25
thank you for my freedom.

OLIVIA.   Oh Heavens, that voice!

ZORIANA.   Gentle Christian, perhaps I have over-stepped the bounds
prescribed my sex. I was early taught a love of Christianity, but I
must now confess, my actions are impelled by a tenderer passion.   30

HENRY.   That passion which you have so generously avowed has
excited my utmost gratitude, and I only wish for power to con-
vince you, how much you have bound me to your service.

OLIVIA.   Oh! (*Faints.*)

ZORIANA.   What ails my friend? Help me to support her; she is an   35
amiable creature and will accompany us in our flight. She revives;
how are you? Speak; my Olivia.

HENRY.   Olivia, did you say?

OLIVIA.   Yes, Henry, your forsaken Olivia.

HENRY.   Oh my beloved! Is it possible that I see you here in bond-   40
age? Where is your father?

OLIVIA.   In bondage too—but, Henry, you had forgot me; you
could renounce your vows and wed another.

HENRY.   Oh no; never for one moment has my thoughts strayed
from my Olivia—I never regretted slavery, but as it deprived me   45
of your sweet converse, nor wished for freedom, but to ratify my
vows to you.

ZORIANA.   (*Aside.*)   How? Mutual lovers! My disappointed heart
beats high with resentment, but in vain; I wish to be a Christian,
and I will, though my heart breaks, perform a Christian's duty.   50

HENRY.   Pardon, beauteous lady, an involuntary error. I have long
loved this Christian maid; we are betrothed to each other. This
evening I obeyed your summons, to inform you that grateful
thanks and fervent prayers were all the return I could make for
the unmerited kindness you have shown me.   55

OLIVIA.   Generous Zoriana, blame not my Henry.

ZORIANA.   Think not so meanly of me, as to suppose I live but for
myself—that I loved your Henry, I can without a blush avow,
but, 'twas a love so pure, that to see him happy will gratify my
utmost wish; I still rejoice that I've procured his liberty; you shall   60

with him embrace the opportunity, and be henceforth as blest—
(*Aside.*) as I am wretched.

HENRY. You will go with us.

ZORIANA. Perhaps I may—but let us now separate; tomorrow, from
65 the lattice, you shall receive instructions how to proceed: in the
meantime here is more gold and jewels. I never knew their value,
till I found they could ransom you from slavery.

HENRY. Words are poor.

ZORIANA. Leave us. My heart's oppressed, I wish to be alone; doubt
70 not the safety of your Olivia; she must be safe with me, for she
is dear to you.

(*Henry kisses her hand, bows and exits. They stand sometime without
speaking.*)

ZORIANA. Olivia!

OLIVIA. Madam!

ZORIANA. Why are you silent, do you doubt my sincerity?

75 OLIVIA. Oh no—but I was thinking, if we should fail in our
attempt; if we should be taken—

ZORIANA. Gracious heaven forbid!

OLIVIA. Who then could deprecate[1] your father's wrath? Yourself,
my Henry, and my dearest father, all, all, would fall a sacrifice.

80 ZORIANA. These are groundless fears.

OLIVIA. Perhaps they are; but yet, I am resolved to stay behind.

ZORIANA. Do not think of it.

OLIVIA. Forgive me; I am determined, and that so firmly, it will be
in vain to oppose me. If you escape—the Power who protects
85 you, will also give to me the means of following; should you be
taken, I may perhaps move the Dey to forgive you, and even
should my prayers and tears have no effect, my life shall pay the
forfeiture of yours.

ZORIANA. I will not go.

90 OLIVIA. Yes, gentle lady, yes; you must go with them; perhaps you
think it will be a painful task to meet your father's anger; but

---

1 *deprecate* Alleviate.

indeed it will not. The thought of standing forth the preserver of the dear author of my being, of the man who loves me next to heaven, of the friend who could sacrifice her own happiness to mine, would fill my soul with such delight, that even death, in its 95 most horrid shape, could not disturb its tranquility.

ZORIANA.   But, can you suppose your father, and your lover—

OLIVIA.   You must assist my design, you must tell them I am already at liberty, and in a place of safety; when they discover the deception, be it your task, my gentle Zoriana, to wipe the tear of sorrow 100 from their eyes. Be a daughter to my poor father, comfort his age, be kind and tender to him, let him not feel the loss of his Olivia. Be to my Henry (Oh! my bursting heart) a friend, to soothe him in his deep affliction; pour consolation on his wounded mind, and love him if you can, as I have done. 105

(*Exit.*)

ACT 2, SCENE 2

(*Dawn of the day. Another part of the garden—with an alcove. Enter Frederic.*)

FREDERIC.   What a poor unfortunate dog I am; last night I slipped into the garden behind Henry, in hopes I should find some distressed damsel, who wanted a knight-errant to deliver her from captivity; and here have I wandered through windings, turnings, alleys, and labyrinths, till the Devil himself could not find the 5 way out again: someone approaches—by all that's lovely 'tis a woman—young, and handsome too, health glows upon her cheek, and good humour sparkles in her eye; I'll conceal myself, that I may not alarm her.

(*Exit into the alcove.*)

(*Enter Fetnah.*)

FETNAH.

SONG.

10   Aurora,[1] lovely blooming fair,
        Unbarred the eastern skies;
        While many a soft pellucid tear,
        Ran trickling from her eyes.
        Onward she came, with heart-felt glee,
15   Leading the dancing hours;
        For though she wept, she smiled to see,
        Her tears refresh the flowers.
        Phoebus,[2] who long her charms admired,
        With bright refulgent ray;
20   Came forth, and as the maid retired,
        He kissed her tears away.

What a sweet morning, I could not sleep, so the moment the
doors were open, I came out to try and amuse myself. 'Tis a
delightful garden, but I believe I should hate the finest place in
25   the world, if I was obliged to stay in it, whether I would or no.
If I am forced to remain here much longer, I shall fret myself as
old and as ugly as Mustapha. That's no matter; there's nobody
here to look at one, but great, black, goggle-eyed creatures, that
are posted here and there to watch us. And when one speaks to
30   them, they shake their frightful heads, and make such a horrid
noise—lord, I wish I could run away, but that's impossible; there
is no getting over these nasty high walls. I do wish some dear,
sweet, Christian man, would fall in love with me, break open the
garden gates, and carry me off.

35 FREDERIC.   (*Stealing out.*)   Say you so my charmer, then I'm your
    man.

    FETNAH.   And take me to that charming place, where there are no
        bolts and bars; no mutes[3] and guards; no bow-strings and scimi-
        tars. Oh! It must be a dear delightful country, where women do
40   just what they please.

---

1   *Aurora*   In Roman mythology, the goddess of the dawn.

2   *Phoebus*   Name applied to the Greek god Apollo in his role as sun god.

3   *mutes*   Term formerly used to refer to deaf people employed in Turkish and Algerian courts
    on account of their discretion.

36   SUSANNA HASWELL ROWSON

FREDERIC.   I'm sure you are a dear, delightful creature.

([*Fetnah,*] *turning, sees him, and shrieks.*)

FREDERIC.   Hush, my sweet little infidel, or we shall be discovered.

FETNAH.   Why, who are you, and how came you here?

FREDERIC.   I am a poor forlorn fellow, beautiful creature, over head and ears in love with you, and I came here to tell you how much   45
I adore you.

FETNAH.   (*Aside.*) Oh dear! what a charming man. I do wish he would run away with me.

FREDERIC.   Perhaps this is the lady who wrote to Henry; she looks like a woman of quality, if I may judge from her dress. I'll ask her.   50
You wish to leave this country, lovely Moor?

FETNAH.   Lord, I'm not a Moriscan; I hate 'em all, there is nothing I wish so much as to get away from them.

FREDERIC.   Your letters said so.

FETNAH.   Letters!   55

FREDERIC.   Yes, the letters you dropped from the window upon the terrace.

FETNAH.   (*Aside.*) He takes me for some other, I'll not undeceive him, and maybe, he'll carry [me] off. Yes, sir; yes, I did write to you.   60

FREDERIC.   To me!

FETNAH.   To be sure; did you think it was to anybody else?

FREDERIC.   Why, there has been a small mistake.

FETNAH.   (*Aside.*) And there's like to be a greater if you knew all.

FREDERIC.   And do you indeed love me?   65

FETNAH.   Yes, I do, better than anybody I ever saw in my life.

FREDERIC.   And if I can get you out of the palace, you will go away with me?

FETNAH.   To be sure I will, that's the very thing I wish.

FREDERIC.   Oh! thou sweet, bewitching, little—   70

(*Catching her in his arms.*)

MULEY MOLOC.   (*Without.*) Tell him Fetnah shall be sent home to him immediately.

FETNAH.   Oh lord! what will become of us? That's my lord the
    Dey—you'll certainly be taken.
75 FREDERIC.   Yes, I feel the bow-string round my neck already; what
    shall I do—where shall I hide?
FETNAH.   Stay, don't be frightened—I'll bring you off; catch me in
    your arms again.

(*She throws herself in his arms as though fainting.*)

(*Enter Muley Moloc and Mustapha.*)

MULEY MOLOC.   I tell thee, Mustapha, I cannot banish the beauti-
80   ful Christian one moment from my thoughts. The women seem
    all determined to perplex me; I was pleased with the beauty of
    Fetnah, but her childish caprice—
MUSTAPHA.   Behold, my lord, the fair slave you mention, in the
    arms of a stranger.
85 FREDERIC.   (*Aside.*) Now, good-bye to poor Pil-garlic.[1]
FETNAH.   (*Pretending to recover.*) Are they gone, and am I safe? Oh!
    Courteous stranger, when the Dey my master knows—
MULEY MOLOC.   What's the matter Fetnah; who is this slave?
FETNAH.   (*Kneeling.*) Oh mighty prince, this stranger has preserved
90   me from the greatest outrage.
MULEY MOLOC.   What outrage?
FETNAH.   Now, do not look angry at your poor little slave, who,
    knowing she had offended you, could not rest, and came early
    into the garden to lament her folly.
95 FREDERIC.   (*Aside.*) Well said, woman.
MULEY MOLOC.   Rise, Fetnah; we have forgot your rashness—
    proceed.
FETNAH.   So, as I was sitting, melancholy and sad, in the alcove, I
    heard a great noise, and presently four or five Turks leaped over
100   the wall, and began to plunder the garden. I screamed; did not
    you hear me, Mustapha?
FREDERIC.   (*Aside.*) Well said, again.

---

1   *Pil-garlic*   Bald, slovenly, or foolish person; the term was often used self-pityingly (as here),
    meaning "poor foolish me."

FETNAH.   But, the moment they saw me, they seized me, and would
have forced me away, had not this gallant stranger run to my assis-
tance. They, thinking they were pursued by many, relinquished 105
their hold and left me fainting in the stranger's arms.

MULEY MOLOC.   'Tis well.

MUSTAPHA.   But, gracious sir, how came the stranger here?

FREDERIC.   (*Aside.*) Oh! Confound your inquisitive tongue.

MULEY MOLOC.   Aye, Christian; how came you in this garden?   110

FETNAH.   He came from my father. Did not you say my father sent
you here?

FREDERIC.   (*Bows. Aside.*) Now, who the devil is her father?

FETNAH.   He came to beg leave to gather some herbs for a salad,
while they were still fresh with morning dew.   115

FREDERIC.   (*Aside.*) Heaven bless her invention!

MULEY MOLOC.   Go to your apartment.

FETNAH.   Oh dear! If he should ask him any questions when I am
gone, what will become of him?

(*Exit Fetnah.*)

MULEY MOLOC.   Christian, gather the herbs you came for, and 120
depart in peace. Mustapha, go to my daughter Zoriana; tell her
I'll visit her some two hours hence, 'till when, I'll walk in the
refreshing morning air.

(*Exit Muley and Mustapha.*)

FREDERIC.   (*Solus.*) Thanks to dear little infidel's ready wit; I breathe
again. Good Mr. Whiskers,[1] I am obliged by your dismission of 125
me—I will depart as fast as I can; and yet I cannot but regret leaving my lovely little Moor behind. Who comes here? The apostate[2]
Hassan. Now could I swear some mischief was afoot. I'll keep out
of sight and try to learn his business.

(*Frederic retires.*)

---

1   *Mr. Whiskers*   I.e., Muley Moloc.
2   *apostate*   One who has abandoned one's religion.

(*Enter Ben Hassan and Mustapha.*)

130 BEN HASSAN.   Indeed, I am vashtly sorry that my daughter has
offended my good lord the Dey; but if he will admit me to his
sublime presence, I can give him intelligence of so important a
nature, as I makes no doubt will incline him to pardon her, for
my sake.

135 MUSTAPHA.   I will tell him you wait his leisure.

(*Exit Mustapha.*)

FREDERIC.   The traitor is on the point of betraying us. I must if
possible prevent his seeing the Dey. (*Runs to Ben Hassan with all
the appearance of violent terror.*) Oh! my dear friend Hassan, for
heaven's sake what brought you here? Don't you know the Dey is so
140   highly offended with you that he vows to have you impaled alive?
BEN HASSAN.   Oh dear! Mr. Frederic, how did you know?
FREDERIC.   It was by the luckiest chance in the world; I happened to
be in this garden when I overheard a slave of yours informing the
Dey that you had not only amassed immense riches, which you
145   intended to carry out of his territories; but, that you had many
valuable slaves, which you kept concealed from him, that you
might reap the benefit of their ransom.
BEN HASSAN.   Oh, what will become of me! But, come, come; Mr.
Frederic, you only say this to frighten me.
150 FREDERIC.   Well, you'll see that; for I heard him command his
guards to be ready to seize you when he gave the signal, as he
expected you here every moment.
BEN HASSAN.   Oh! What shall I do?
FREDERIC.   If you stay here, you will certainly be bastinadoed—
155   impaled—burnt.
BEN HASSAN.   Oh dear! Oh dear!
FREDERIC.   Make haste my dear friend; run home as fast as possible;
hide your treasure and keep out of the way.
BEN HASSAN.   Oh dear! I wish I was safe in Duke's Place.[1]

(*Exit.*)

---

1   *Duke's Place*   Area of London known for its Jewish community.

FREDERIC.   Let me but get you once safe into your own house, and 160
I'll prevent your betraying us I'll warrant.

(*Exit.*)

ACT 2, SCENE 3

(*Fetnah's Apartment. [Enter] Fetnah and Selima.*)

FETNAH.   Now will you pretend to say you are happy here, and that
you love the Dey.

SELIMA.   I have been here many years; the Dey has been very good
to me, and my chief employment has been to wait on his daughter, Zoriana, till I was appointed to attend you. To you perhaps, 5
he may be an object of disgust; but, looking up to him as a kind
and generous master, to me he appears amiable.

FETNAH.   Oh! To be sure, he is a most amiable creature; I think I
see him now, seated on his cushion, a bowl of sherbet by his side,
and a long pipe in his mouth. Oh! How charmingly the tobacco 10
must perfume his whiskers—here, Mustapha, says he, "Go, bid
the slave Selima come to me." Well it does not signify, that word
"slave" does so stick in my throat—I wonder how any woman of
spirit can gulp it down.

SELIMA.   We are accustomed to it. 15

FETNAH.   The more's the pity: for how sadly depressed must the soul
be, to whom custom has rendered bondage supportable.

SELIMA.   Then, if opportunity offered, you would leave Algiers?

FETNAH.   That I would, most cheerfully.

SELIMA.   And perhaps, bestow your affections on some young 20
Christian.

FETNAH.   That you may be sure of; for say what you will, I am sure
the woman must be blind and stupid, who would not prefer a
young, handsome, good-humoured Christian, to an old, ugly,
ill-natured Turk. 25

(*Enter Sadi—with robe, turban, etc.*)

FETNAH.   Well, what's your business?

SADI.   I—I—I—I'm afraid I'm wrong.

SELIMA.   Who sent you here?

SADI.   I was told to take these to our master's son, young Soliman. But somehow, in the turnings and windings in this great house, I believe I have lost myself.

SELIMA.   You have mistaken—

FETNAH.   Mistaken—no, he is very right; here, give me the clothes, I'll take care of them, (*Takes them.*) there, there, go about your business, it's all very well.

(*Exit Sadi.*)

Now, Selima, I'll tell you what I'll do; I'll put these on—go to the Dey, and see if he will know me.

SELIMA.   He'll be angry.

FETNAH.   Pshaw! You're so fearful of his anger. If you let the men see you are afraid of them, they'll hector and domineer finely. No, no, let them think you don't care whether they are pleased or no, and then they'll be as condescending and humble. Go, go—take the clothes into the next apartment.

(*Exit Selima.*)

Now, if by means of these clothes, I can get out of the palace, I'll seek the charming young Christian I saw this morning. We'll get my dear instructress from my father's and fly together from this land of captivity to the regions of Peace and Liberty.

(*Exit.*)

ACT 3, SCENE 1

(*A kind of grotto. [Enter] Frederic, Henry, Sebastian, and Slaves.*)

SEBASTIAN.   Now, if you had trusted me at first, I'll answer for it, I had got you all safe out; aye, and that dear, sweet creature, madam Zoriana too! What a pity it is she's Mahometan, your true bred Mahometans never drink any wine. Now, for my part,

I like a drop of good liquor, it makes a body feel so comfortable, 5
so ... so, I don't know howish, as if they were friends with all the
world—I always keep a friend or two hid here. (*Takes out some
bottles.*) Mum, don't be afraid, they are no tell-tales—only when
they are trusted too far.

FREDERIC.   Well, Sebastian, don't be too unguarded in trusting these 10
very good friends tonight.

SEBASTIAN.   Never fear me; did not I tell you I'd show you a place
of safety; well, haven't I performed my promise? When I first
discovered this cave, or cavern, or grotto, or cell, or whatever
your fine-spoken folks may call it; this, said I, would be a good 15
place to hide people in. So I never told my master.

HENRY.   This fellow will do some mischief, with his non-sensical
prate.[1]

FREDERIC.   I don't fear him, he has an honest heart, hid under an
appearance of ignorance. It grows duskish, Sebastian, have we 20
good sentinels placed at the entrance of the cell?

SEBASTIAN.   Good sentinels! Why do you suppose I would trust any
with that post but those I could depend on?

HENRY.   Two hours past midnight we must invest[2] the garden of the
Dey; I have here a letter from Zoriana, which says she will at that 25
time be ready to join us—and lead us to the prison of my Olivia's
father. Olivia is by some means already at liberty.

SENTINEL.   (*Without.*) You must not not pass.

FETNAH.   No—but I must. I have business.

SEBASTIAN.   What, what, what's all this? 30

(*Exit.*)

FETNAH.   Nay, for pity's sake, don't kill me.

(*Re-enter Sebastian, forcing in Fetnah habited[3] like a boy.*)

SEBASTIAN.   No, no, we won't kill you; we'll only make you a slave,
and you know that's nothing.

---

1   *prate*   Talk.
2   *invest*   Surround.
3   *habited*   Dressed.

FETNAH.   (*Aside.*) There is my dear Christian, but I won't discover
35   myself, till I try if he will know me.
HENRY.   Who are you, young man and for what purpose were you
     loitering about this place?
FETNAH.   I am Soliman, son to the Dey, and I heard by chance that a
     band of slaves had laid a plot to invest the palace, and so I traced
40   some of them to this cell and was just going—
FIRST SLAVE.   To betray us.
SECOND SLAVE.   Let us dispatch him, and instantly disperse till the
     appointed hour.
SEVERAL SLAVES.   Aye, let us kill him.
45 HENRY.   Hold; why should we harm this innocent youth?
FIRST SLAVE.   He would be the means of our suffering most cruel
     tortures.
HENRY.   True, but he is now in our power: young, innocent, and
     unprotected. Oh my friends! Let us not, on this auspicious night,
50   when we hope to emancipate ourselves from slavery, tinge the
     bright standard[1] of liberty with blood.
SLAVES.   'Tis necessary; our safety demands it.

(*They rush on Fetnah; in her struggle her turban falls off—she breaks
from them and runs to Frederic.*)

FETNAH.   Save me, dear Christian! It's only poor little Fetnah.
FREDERIC.   Save you my sweet little infidel—why, I'll impale the
55   wretch, who should move but a finger against you.
SEBASTIAN.   Oh! Oh! a mighty pretty boy to be sure.
FREDERIC.   But tell me—how got you out of the palace, and how
     did you discover us?
FETNAH.   I have not time now, but this I will assure you, I came with
60   a full intention to go with you, if you will take me, the whole
     world over.
FREDERIC.   Can you doubt—
FETNAH.   Doubt, no to be sure I don't, but you must comply with
     one request, before we depart.
65 FREDERIC.   Name it.

---

1   *standard*   Flag.

FETNAH. I have a dear friend, who is a captive at my father's; she must be released, or Fetnah cannot be happy, even with the man she loves.

([*Fetnah*] *draws aside and confers with Henry.*)

SEBASTIAN. Well, here am I, Sebastian; who have been a slave, two years, six months, a fortnight and three days, and have, all that 70 time worked in the garden of the Alcaide,[1] who has twelve wives, thirty concubines, and two pretty daughters; and yet not one of the insensible hussies ever took a fancy to me. 'Tis devilish hard, that when I go home, I can't say to my honoured father, the barber, and to my reverend mother, the laundress: this is 75 the beautiful princess who fell in love with me; jumped over the garden-wall of his serene holiness her father, and ran away with your dutiful son, Sebastian—then, falling on my knees—thus.

HENRY. What's the matter, Sebastian? There is no danger, don't be afraid, man. 80

FREDERIC. Sebastian, you must take a party of our friends, go to the house of Ben Hassan, and bring from thence an American lady. I have good reason to think you will meet with no opposition; she may be at first unwilling to come, but tell her—friends and countrymen await her here. 85

FETNAH. Tell her, her own Fetnah expects her.

FREDERIC. Treat her with all imaginable respect: Go, my good Sebastian; be diligent, silent, and expeditious. You, my dear Fetnah, I will place in an inner part of the grotto, where you will be safe, while we effect the escape of Olivia's father. 90

FETNAH. What, shut me up! Do you take me for a coward?

HENRY. We respect you as a woman and would shield you from danger.

FETNAH. A woman! Why, so I am; but in the cause of love or friendship, a woman can face danger with as much spirit, and as little 95 fear, as the bravest man amongst you. Do you lead the way, I'll follow to the end.

---

1 *Alcaide* Commander of a fortress or prison warden.

(*Exit Fetnah, Frederic, Henry, etc.*)

SEBASTIAN. (*Solus.*) Bravo! Excellent! Bravissimo! Why, 'tis a little
body; but ecod,[1] she's a devil of a spirit. It's a fine thing to meet
100   with a woman that has a little fire in her composition. I never
much liked your milk-and-water ladies; to be sure, they are easily
managed—but your spirited lasses require taming; they make a
man look about him—dear, sweet, angry creatures, here's their
health. This is the summum-bonum[2] of all good: If they are kind,
105   this, this, makes them appear angels and goddesses: If they are
saucy, why then, here, here, in this we'll drown the remembrance
of the bewitching, froward,[3] little devils. In all kind of difficulties
and vexations, nothing helps the invention, or cheers the courage, like a drop from the jorum.[4]

SONG.

110   When I was a poor, little innocent boy,
About sixteen or eighteen years old;
At Susan and Marian I cast a sheep's eye,
But Susan was saucy and Marian was shy;
So I flirted with Flora, with Cecily and Di.
115   But they too, were frumpish and cold.
Says Diego, one day, what ails you I pray?
I fetched a deep sigh—Diego, says I,
Women hate me. Oh! how I adore 'em.
Pho;° nonsense, said he,   *pshaw (dismissive sound)*
never mind it my lad.
120   Hate you? Then hate them boy, come, never be sad,
Here, take a good sup of the jorum.
If they're foolish and mulish, refuse you, abuse you,
No longer pursue,
They'll soon buckle too
125   When they find they're neglected,

---

1   *ecod*   Variant of the oath "by God!"
2   *summum-bonum*   Latin: highest good.
3   *froward*   Difficult to manage.
4   *jorum*   Drinking cup.

Old maids, unprotected,
Ah! then 'tis their turn to woo;
But bid them defiance, and form an alliance,
With the mirth-giving, care-killing jorum.
I took his advice, but was sent to the war,   130
And soon I was called out to battle;
I heard the drums beat, Oh! how great was my fear,
I wished myself sticking, aye, up to each ear
In a horse-pond—and skulked away into the rear.
When the cannon and bombs 'gan to rattle,   135
Said I to myself, you're a damned foolish elf,
Sebastian keep up, then I took a good sup.
Turkish villains, shall we fly before 'em;
What, give it up tamely and yield ourselves slaves,
To a pack of rapscallions, vile infidel knaves,   140
Then I kissed the sweet lips of my jorum.
No, hang 'em, we'll bang 'em, and rout 'em, and scout 'em.
If we but pursue,
They must buckle too:
Ah! then without wonder,   145
I heard the loud thunder,
Of cannon and musketry too,
But bid them defiance, being firm in alliance,
With the courage-inspiring jorum.

(*Exit.*)

ACT 3, SCENE 2

(*Ben Hassan's house.* [*Enter*] *Rebecca and Augustus.*)

AUGUSTUS.   Dear mother, don't look so sorrowful; my master is not
   very hard with me. Do, pray, be happy.
REBECCA.   Alas! My dear Augustus, can I be happy while you are a
   slave? My own bondage is nothing. But you, my child—
AUGUSTUS.   Nay, mother, don't mind it; I am but a boy you know.   5
   If I was a man—
REBECCA.   What would you do my love?

AUGUSTUS.   I'd stamp beneath my feet the wretch that would enslave
my mother.

10 REBECCA.   There burst forth the sacred flame which heaven itself
fixed in the human mind; Oh! my brave boy! (*Embracing him.*)
Ever may you preserve that independent spirit, that dares assert
the rights of the oppressed, by power unawed, unchecked by
servile fear.

15 AUGUSTUS.   Fear, mother? What should I be afraid of? Ain't I an
American, and I am sure you have often told me, in a right cause
the Americans did not fear anything.

(*Enter Ben Hassan.*)

BEN HASSAN.   So, here's a piece of vork; I'se be like to have fine deal
of troubles on your account. Oh! that ever I should run the risk
20 of my life by keeping you concealed from the Dey.
REBECCA.   If I am a trouble to you, if my being here endangers your
life, why do you not send me away?
BEN HASSAN.   There be no ships here for you to go in; besides, who
will pay me?
25 REBECCA.   Indeed, if you will send me to my native land, I will
faithfully remit to you my ransom; aye, double what you have
required.
BEN HASSAN.   If I thought I could depend—

(*Enter Servant.*)

SERVANT.   Sir, your house is surrounded by armed men.
30 BEN HASSAN.   What, Turks?
SERVANT.   Slaves, sir; many of whom I have seen in the train of the
Dey.
BEN HASSAN.   Vhat do they vant?
SERVANT.   One of my companions asked them, and received for
35 answer, they would shew us presently.
SEBASTIAN.   (*Without.*) Stand away, fellow; I will search the house.
REBECCA.   Oh heavens! What will become of me?
BEN HASSAN.   What will become of me? Oh! I shall be impaled,
burnt, bastinadoed, murdered, where shall I hide, how shall I
40 escape them?

(Runs through a door, as though into another apartment.)

SEBASTIAN.   (*Without.*) This way, friends; this way.

REBECCA.   Oh, my child, we are lost!

AUGUSTUS.   Don't be frightened, mother, through this door is a way
into the garden. If I had but a sword, boy as I am, I'd fight for
you till I died.   45

(Exit with Rebecca.)

(Enter Sebastian etc.)

SEBASTIAN.   I thought I heard voices this way; now my friends, the
lady we seek, is a most lovely, amiable creature, whom we must
accost with respect and convey hence in safety. She is a woman
of family and fortune and is highly pleased with my person and
abilities; let us therefore, search every cranny of the house till we   50
find her; she may not recollect me directly, but never mind, we
will carry her away first and assure her of her safety afterwards.
Go search the rooms in that wing, I will myself investigate the
apartments on this side.

(Exit Slaves.)

Well I have made these comrades of mine believe I am a favoured   55
lover in pursuit of a kind mistress, that's something for them to
talk of; and I believe many a fine gentleman is talked of for love
affairs that has as little foundation; and so one is but talked of
as a brave or gallant man, what signifies whether there is any
foundation for it or no. And yet, hang it, who knows but I may   60
prove it a reality. If I release this lady from captivity, she may cast
an eye of affection—may—why I dare say she will. I am but poor
Sebastian, the barber of Cordova's son, 'tis true; but I am well
made, very well made. My leg is not amiss—then I can make a
graceful bow. And as to polite compliments, let me but find her,   65
and I'll show them what it is to have a pretty person, a graceful
air, and a smooth tongue. But I must search this apartment.

(Exit.)

Act 3, Scene 3

(*Another apartment. Enter Ben Hassan with a petticoat and robe on, a bonnet, and deep veil in his hand.*)

BEN HASSAN.   I think now, they vill hardly know me, in my vife's clothes; I could not find a turban, but this head dress of Rebecca's vill do better, because it vill hide my face—but, how shall I hide my monies? I've got a vast deal, in bills of exchange and all kinds
5   of paper; if I can but get safe off with this book in my pocket, I shall have enough to keep me easy as long as I live.

(*Puts it in his pocket and drops it.*)

Oh! This is a judgment fallen upon me for betraying the Christians.

(*Noise without.*)

Oh lord! Here they come.

(*Ties on the bonnet and retires into one corner of the apartment.*)

(*Enter Sebastian etc.*)

10 SEBASTIAN.   There she is, I thought I traced the sweep of her train this way. Don't mind her struggles or entreaties but bring her away. Don't be alarmed, madam, you will meet with every attention, you will be treated with the greatest respect, and let me whisper to you there is more happiness in store for you, than you
15 can possibly imagine. Friends, convey her gently to the appointed place.

(*They take up Ben Hassan and carry him off.*)

BEN HASSAN.   Oh!—o—o—o!

(*Exit.*)

(*Enter Augustus and Rebecca.*)

AUGUSTUS. See, my dear mother, there is no one here, they are all
gone; it was not you they came to take away.

REBECCA. It is for you, I fear, more than for myself. I do not think 20
you are safe with me—go, my beloved, return to your master.

AUGUSTUS. What, go and leave my mother without a protector?

REBECCA. Alas, my love, you are not able to protect yourself. And
your staying here only adds to my distress. Leave me for the
present. I hope the period is not far off, when we shall never be 25
separated.

AUGUSTUS. Mother! Dear mother! My heart is so big it almost
chokes me. Oh! how I wish I was a man.

(*Exit Augustus.*)

REBECCA. (*Solus.*) Heaven guard my precious child! I cannot think
him quite safe anywhere, but with me, his danger would be 30
imminent. The emotions of his heart hang on his tongue, and the
least outrage offered to his mother he would resent at peril of his
life. My spirits are oppressed—I have a thousand fears for him,
and for myself. The house appears deserted—all is silent—what's
this? 35

(*Takes up the pocket-book.*)

Oh heaven! Is it possible! Bills, to the amount of my own ransom
and many others—transporting thought! My son—my darling
boy, this would soon emancipate you! Here's a letter addressed
to me—the money is my own. Oh joy beyond expression! My
child will soon be free. I have also the means of cheering many 40
children of affliction with the blest sound of liberty. Hassan, you
have dealt unjustly by me, but I forgive you—for, while my own
heart overflows with gratitude for this unexpected blessing, I will
wish every human being as happy as I am this moment.

(*Exit.*)

Act 3, Scene 4

(*Dey's garden.* [*Enter*] *Zoriana.*)

ZORIANA.   (*Solus.*) How vain are the resolves, how treacherous the
heart of a woman in love; but a few hours since, I thought I could
have cheerfully relinquished the hope of having my tenderness
returned; and found a relief from my own sorrow in reflecting
5   on the happiness of Henry and Olivia. Then why does this selfish
heart beat with transport at the thought of their separation? Poor
Olivia—how deep must be her affliction. Ye silent shades, scenes
of content and peace, how sad would you appear to the poor
wretch who wandered here, the victim of despair. But the fond
10   heart, glowing with all the joys of mutual love, delighted views
the beauties scattered round, thinks every flower is sweet, and
every prospect gay.

SONG.

In lowly cot° or mossy cell,   *cottage*
With harmless nymphs and rural swains,[1]
15   'Tis there contentment loves to dwell,
'Tis there soft peace and pleasure reigns;
But even there, the heart may prove,
The pangs of disappointed love.
But softly, hope persuading,
20   Forbids me long to mourn;
My tender heart pervading,
Portends my love's return.
Ah! then how bright and gay,
Appears the rural scene,
25   More radiant breaks the day,
The night is more serene.

(*Enter Henry.*)

---

1   *nymphs ... swains* A nymph is a sexually desirable young woman; a swain is a young male
suitor. The terms are commonly used to refer to lovers in pastoral poetry.

HENRY. Be not alarmed, madam. I have ventured here earlier than I intended, to enquire how my Olivia effected her escape.

ZORIANA. This letter will inform you—but, early as it is, the palace is wrapped in silence. My father is retired to rest. Follow me, and 30 I will conduct you to the old man's prison.

HENRY. Have you the keys?

ZORIANA. I have; follow in silence, the least alarm would be fatal to our purpose.

(*Exit.*)

ACT 3, SCENE 5

(*The grotto again. [Enter] Sebastian, leading in Ben Hassan.*)

SEBASTIAN. Beautiful creature, don't be uneasy, I have risked my life to procure your liberty, and will at the utmost hazard convey you to your desired home: but, Oh! most amiable—most divine— most delicate lady, suffer me thus humbly on my knees to confess my adoration of you; to solicit your pity, and— 5

BEN HASSAN. (*In a feigned tone.*) I pray tell me why you brought me from the house of the good Ben Hassan, and where you design to take me.

SEBASTIAN. Oh! thou adorable, be not offended at my presump- tion, but having an opportunity of leaving this place of captivity, 10 I was determined to take you with me, and prevent your falling into the power of the Dey, who would no doubt be in raptures, should he behold your exquisite beauty. Sweet innocent charmer, permit your slave to remove the envious curtain that shades your enchanting visage. 15

BEN HASSAN. Oh no! Not for the world; I have in consideration of many past offences, resolved to take the veil and hide myself from mankind for ever.

SEBASTIAN. That my dear, sweet creature, would be the highest offence you could commit. Women were never made, with all 20 their prettiness and softness, and bewitching ways, to be hid from us men, who came into the world for no other purpose, than to see, admire, love and protect them. Come, I must have a peep under that curtain; I long to see your dear little sparkling eyes, your lovely blooming cheeks—and I am resolved to taste your cherry lips.

25

(In struggling to kiss him, the bonnet falls off.)

Why, what in the devil's name, have we here?

BEN HASSAN.   Only a poor old woman—who has been in captivity—

SEBASTIAN.   These fifty years at least, by the length of your beard.

30

FREDERIC.   (*Without.*) Sebastian—bring the lady to the waterside, and wait till we join you.

BEN HASSAN.   I wish I was in any safe place.

SEBASTIAN.   Oh ma'am, you are in no danger anywhere—come make haste.

35

BEN HASSAN.   But give me my veil again, if anyone saw my face it would shock me.

SEBASTIAN.   And damme,[1] but I think it would shock them—here, take your curtain, though I think to be perfectly safe, you had best go barefaced.

40

BEN HASSAN.   If you hurry me I shall faint; consider the delicacy of my nerves.

SEBASTIAN.   Come along, there's no time for fainting now.

BEN HASSAN.   The respect due—

SEBASTIAN.   To old age—I consider it all—you are very respectable. Oh! Sebastian what a cursed ninny you were to make so much fuss about a woman old enough to be your grandmother.

45

(Exit.)

ACT 3, SCENE 6

(Inside the Palace. [Enter] Muley Moloc and Mustapha.)

MULEY MOLOC.   Fetnah gone, Zoriana gone … and the fair slave Olivia?

---

1   *damme*   I.e., damn me.

MUSTAPHA. All, dread[1] sir.

MULEY MOLOC. Send instantly to the prison of the slave Constant. 'Tis he who has again plotted to rob me of Olivia. 5

(*Exit Mustapha.*)

My daughter, too, he has seduced from her duty. But he shall not escape my vengeance.

(*Re-enter Mustapha.*)

MUSTAPHA. Some of the fugitives are overtaken and wait in chains without.

MULEY MOLOC. Is Zoriana taken? 10

MUSTAPHA. Your daughter is safe. The old man, too, is taken, but Fetnah and Olivia have escaped.

MULEY MOLOC. Bring in the wretches.

(*Henry, Constant, and several Slaves brought in, chained.*)

Rash old man, how have you dared to tempt your fate again? Do you not know the torments that await the Christian who 15 attempts to rob the harem of a Mussulman?[2]

CONSTANT. I know you have the power to end my being, but that's a period[3] I more wish than fear.

MULEY MOLOC. Where is Olivia?

CONSTANT. Safe, I hope, beyond your power. Oh, gracious heaven, 20 protect my darling from this tyrant, and let my life pay the dear purchase of her freedom.

MULEY MOLOC. Bear them to the torture. Who and what am I, that a vile slave dares brave me to my face?

HENRY. Hold off! We know that we must die, and we are prepared 25 to meet our fate like men. Impotent, vain boaster, call us not slaves. You are a slave indeed, to rude, ungoverned passion, to pride, to avarice and lawless love. Exhaust your cruelty in finding

---

1 *dread* Revered.
2 *Mussulman* Muslim.
3 *period* End.

tortures for us, and we will smiling tell you the blow that ends
our lives strikes off our chains and sets our souls at liberty.

MULEY MOLOC.   Hence! Take them from my sight.

(*Captives taken off.*)

Devise each means of torture. Let them linger months, years,
ages, in their misery.

(*Enter Olivia.*)

OLIVIA.   Stay,[1] Muley, stay. Recall your cruel sentence.

MULEY MOLOC.   Olivia here; is it possible?

OLIVIA.   I have never left the palace. Those men are innocent. So is
your daughter. It is I alone deserve your anger; then on me only
let it fall. It was I procured false keys to the apartments; it was
I seduced your daughter to our interest. I bribed the guards and
with entreaty won the young Christian to attempt to free my
father. Then, since I was the cause of their offenses, it is fit my life
should pay the forfeiture of theirs.

MULEY MOLOC.   Why did you not accompany them?

OLIVIA.   Fearing what has happened, I remained, in hopes, by tears
and supplications, to move you to forgive my father. Oh, Muley,
save his life! Save all his friends, and if you must have blood to
appease your vengeance, let me alone be the sacrifice.

MULEY MOLOC.   (*Aside.*) How her softness melts me.

(*To Olivia.*)

Rise, Olivia. You may on easier terms give them both life and
freedom.

OLIVIA.   No. Here I kneel till you recall your orders. Haste, or it
may be too late.

MULEY MOLOC.   Mustapha, go bid them delay the execution.

(*Exit Mustapha.*)

---

1   *Stay* Stop.

OLIVIA.   Now teach me to secure their lives and freedom, and my last breath shall bless you.   55

MULEY MOLOC.   Renounce your faith. Consent to be my wife. Nay, if you hesitate—

OLIVIA.   I do not. Give me but an hour to think.

MULEY MOLOC.   Not a moment. Determine instantly. Your answer gives them liberty or death.   60

OLIVIA.   Then I am resolved. Swear to me, by Mohammed—an oath I know you Musselmen never violate—that the moment I become your wife my father and his friends are free.

MULEY MOLOC.   By Mohammed I swear, not only to give them life and freedom, but safe conveyance to their desired home.   65

OLIVIA.   I am satisfied. Now leave me to myself a few short moments, that I may calm my agitated spirits and prepare to meet you in the mosque.

MULEY MOLOC.   Henceforth I live but to obey you.

(*Exits.*)

OLIVIA.   On what a fearful precipice I stand. To go forward is ruin,   70
shame and infamy; to recede is to pronounce sentence of death upon my father and my adored Henry. Oh, insupportable! There is one way, and only one, by which I can fulfill my promise to the Dey, preserve my friends, and not abjure my faith. Source of my being, Thou canst read the heart which Thou hast been   75
pleased to try in the school of adversity. Pardon the weakness of an erring mortal, if, rather than behold a father perish—if, rather than devote his friends to death, I cut the thread of my existence and rush unbidden to Thy presence. Yes, I will to the mosque, perform my promise, preserve the valued lives of those I love,   80
then sink at once into the silent grave and bury all my sorrow in oblivion.

(*Exits.*)

Act 3, Scene 7

(*Another apartment. Enter Olivia with Muley Moloc.*)

MULEY MOLOC. Yes, on my life, they are free. In a few moments they will be here.

OLIVIA. Spare me the trial; for the whole world I would not see them now, nor would I have them know at what a price I have secured their freedom.

(*Enter Henry and Constant.*)

CONSTANT. My child—

HENRY. My love—

OLIVIA. My Henry! O my dear father! Pray excuse these tears.

(*Enter Mustapha.*)

MUSTAPHA. Great sir, the mosque is prepared, and the priest waits your pleasure.

MULEY MOLOC. Come, my Olivia.

HENRY. The mosque—the priest—what dreadful sacrifice is then intended?

OLIVIA. Be not alarmed. I must needs attend a solemn rite which gratitude requires—go my dear father—dearest Henry leave me; and be assured, when next you see Olivia, she will be wholly free.

(*Enter Rebecca.*)

REBECCA. Hold for a moment.

MULEY MOLOC. What means this bold intrusion?

REBECCA. Muley, you see before you a woman unused to forms of state, despising titles: I come to offer ransom for six Christian slaves. Waiting your leisure, I was informed a Christian maid, to save her father's life, meant to devote herself a sacrifice to your embraces. I have the means: make your demand of ransom, and set the maid, with those she loves, at liberty.

MULEY MOLOC. Her friends are free already; but for herself, she voluntarily remains with me.

REBECCA. Can you unmoved behold her anguish? Release her Muley. Name but the sum that will pay her ransom, 'tis yours.

MULEY MOLOC. Woman, the wealth of Golconda[1] could not pay her ransom. Can you imagine that I, whose slave she is; I, who could force her obedience to my will and yet gave life and freedom to those Christians to purchase her compliance, would now relinquish her for paltry gold? Contemptible idea. Olivia, I spare you some few moments to your father. Take leave of him, and as you part, remember his life and liberty depends on you.

(*Exits.*)

REBECCA. Poor girl—what can I do to mitigate your sufferings?

OLIVIA. Nothing. My fate, alas, is fixed. But, generous lady, by what name shall we remember you—what nation are you of?

REBECCA. I am an American—but while I only claim kindred with the afflicted, it is of little consequence where I first drew my breath.

CONSTANT. An American—from what state?

REBECCA. New York is my native place; there did I spend the dear delightful days of childhood, and there, alas, I drained the cup of deep affliction, to the very dregs.

CONSTANT. My heart is strangely interested. Dearest lady, will you impart to us your tale of sorrow, that we may mourn with one who feels so much for us?

REBECCA. Early in life, while my brave countrymen were struggling for their freedom,[2] it was my fate to love and be beloved by a young British officer, to whom, though strictly forbid by my father, I was privately married.

CONSTANT. Married! Say you?

REBECCA. My father soon discovered our union; enraged, he spurned me from him, discarded, cursed me, and for four years I followed my husband's fortune. At length my father relented; on a sick bed he sent for me to attend him. I went, taking with me an infant son, leaving my husband and a lovely girl, then scarcely

---

1   *Golconda*   Fort in India. The area surrounding it is famous for its diamond mines, and the name "Golconda" became synonymous with great riches.

2   *struggling for their freedom*   In the American Revolutionary War (1775–83).

three years old. Oh heavens! What sorrows have I known from that unhappy hour. During my absence the armies met—my husband fell—my daughter was torn from me; what then availed the wealth my dying father had bequeathed me? Long—long did I lose all sense of my misery, and returning reason showed me the world only one universal blank. The voice of my darling boy first called me to myself. For him I strove to mitigate my sorrow; for his dear sake I have endured life.

CONSTANT. Pray proceed.

REBECCA. About a year since[1] I heard a rumour that my husband was still alive. Full of the fond hope of again beholding him, I, with my son, embarked for England; but before we reached the coast we were captured by an Algerine.[2]

CONSTANT. Do you think you should recollect your husband?

REBECCA. I think I should, but fourteen years of deep affliction has impaired my memory and may have changed his features.

CONSTANT. What was his name? Oh! speak it quickly!

REBECCA. His name was Constant—but wherefore—

CONSTANT. It was—it was—Rebecca, don't you know me?

REBECCA. Alas—how you are altered. Oh! Constant, why have you forsaken me so long?

CONSTANT. In the battle you mention, I was indeed severely wounded, nay, left for dead in the field; there, my faithful servant found me, when some remaining signs of life encouraged him to attempt my recovery, and by his unremitting care I was at length restored. My first returning thought was fixed on my Rebecca, but after repeated enquiries all I could hear was that your father was dead and yourself and child removed farther from the seat of war. Soon after, I was told you had fallen a martyr to grief for my supposed loss. But see my love, our daughter, our dear Olivia; heaven preserved her to be my comforter.

OLIVIA. (*Kneeling and kissing Rebecca.*) My mother, blessed word. Oh! Do I live to say I have a mother?

REBECCA. Bless you my child, my charming duteous girl; but tell me, by what sad chance you became captives?

---

1 *since* Ago.
2 *Algerine* Algerian pirate ship.

CONSTANT.   After peace was proclaimed with America, my duty
    called me to India, from whence I returned with a ruined consti-   95
    tution. Being advised to try the air of Lisbon, we sailed for that
    place, but Heaven ordained that here, in the land of captivity, I
    should recover a blessing which will amply repay me for all my
    past sufferings.

(*Enter Muley Moloc.*)

MULEY MOLOC.   Christians you trifle with me. Accept your freedom,   100
    go in peace, and leave Olivia to perform her promise. For should
    she waver or draw back, on you I will wreak my vengeance.
REBECCA.   Then let your vengeance fall. We will die together; for
    never shall Olivia, a daughter of Columbia, and a Christian, tar-
    nish her name by apostacy, or live the slave of a despotic tyrant.   105
MULEY MOLOC.   Then take your wish. Who's there?

(*Enter Mustapha hastily.*)

MUSTAPHA.   Arm, mighty sir! The slaves throughout Algiers have
    mutinied—they bear down all before them—this way they
    come—they say, if all the Christian slaves are not immediately
    released, they'll raze the city.   110
REBECCA.   Now! Bounteous heaven, protect my darling boy, and aid
    the cause of freedom.
MULEY MOLOC.   Bear them to instant death.
MUSTAPHA.   Dread sir—consider.
MULEY MOLOC.   Vile abject slave, obey me and be silent! What,   115
    have I power over these Christian dogs, and shall I not exert it?
    Dispatch, I say!

(*Huzza*[1] *and clash of swords without.*)

Why am I not obeyed?

(*Clash again—confused noise—several huzzas.*)

---

1   *Huzza*   Exuberant shout made in unison.

AUGUSTUS.   (*Without.*) Where is my mother? Save, oh! save my
120   mother.
FREDERIC.   (*Speaking.*) Shut up the palace gates, secure the guards,
         and at your peril suffer none to pass.
AUGUSTUS.   (*Entering.*) Oh! Mother are you safe?
CONSTANT.   Bounteous heaven! And am I then restored to more—
125   much more than life—my Rebecca! my children! Oh! This joy is
         more than I can bear.

(*Enter Frederic, Fetnah, Sebastian, Ben Hassan, Slaves, etc.*)

SEBASTIAN.   Great and mighty Ottoman, suffer my friends to show
         you what pretty bracelets these are. Oh, you old dog, we'll give
         you the bastinado presently.
130 FREDERIC.   Forbear Sebastian. Muley Moloc, though your power over
         us is at end, we neither mean to enslave your person, or put a period
         to your existence. We are freemen, and while we assert the rights of
         men, we dare not infringe the privileges of a fellow creature.
SEBASTIAN.   By the law of retaliation, he should be a slave.
135 REBECCA.   By the Christian law, no man should be a slave; it is a
         word so abject, that, but to speak it dyes the cheek with crimson.
         Let us assert our own prerogative, be free ourselves, but let us not
         throw on another's neck the chains we scorn to wear.
SEBASTIAN.   But what must we do with this old gentlewoman?
140 BEN HASSAN.   Oh, pray send me home to Duke's Place.
FREDERIC.   Ben Hassan, your avarice, treachery and cruelty should
         be severely punished; for, if any one deserves slavery, it is he who
         could raise his own fortune on the miseries of others.
BEN HASSAN.   Oh! that I was but crying "old clothes"[1] in the dirtiest
145   alley in London.
FETNAH.   So, you'll leave that poor old man behind?
FREDERIC.   Yes, we leave him to learn humanity.
FETNAH.   (*Going to Ben Hassan.*) Very well, good bye Frederic—
         good bye dear Rebecca: while my father was rich and had friends,
150   I did not much think about my duty; but now he is poor and
         forsaken, I know it too well to leave him alone in his affliction.

---

1   *old clothes*   Street call used by London used-clothing dealers, many of whom were Jewish.

MULEY MOLOC. Stay, Fetnah—Hassan stay. I fear from following the steps of my ancestors, I have greatly erred: teach me then, you who so well know how to practice what is right, how to amend my faults. 155

CONSTANT. Open your prison doors; give freedom to your people. Sink the name of subject in the endearing epithet of fellow-citizen. Then you will be loved and reverenced—then will you find, in promoting the happiness of others, you have secured your own. 160

MULEY MOLOC. Henceforward, then, I will reject all power but such as my united friends shall think me incapable of abusing. Hassan, you are free—to you, my generous conquerors, what can I say?

HENRY. Nothing, but let your future conduct prove how much you 165 value the welfare of your fellow-creatures. Tomorrow we shall leave your capital and return to our native land, where liberty has established her court—where the warlike Eagle extends his glittering pinions in the sunshine of prosperity.

OLIVIA. Long, long, may that prosperity continue. May freedom 170 spread her benign influence through every nation, till the bright Eagle, united with the dove and olive-branch, waves high the acknowledged standard of the world.

EPILOGUE.
WRITTEN AND SPOKEN BY MRS. ROWSON

PROMPTER. (*Behind.*) Come—Mrs. Rowson! Come! Why don't you hurry?

MRS. ROWSON. (*Behind.*) Sir I am here—but I'm in such a flurry, Do let me stop a moment! just for breath,

(*Enter.*)

Bless me! I'm almost terrified to death. 5
Yet sure, I had no real cause for fear,
Since none but liberal, generous friends are here.
Say, will you kindly overlook my errors?
You smile. Then to the winds I give my terrors.

10 Well, ladies, tell me—how d'ye like my play?
"The creature has some sense," methinks you say;
"She says that we should have supreme dominion,
And in good truth, we're all of her opinion.
Women were born for universal sway,
15 Men to adore, be silent, and obey."

True, Ladies—bounteous nature made us fair,
To strew sweet roses round the bed of care.
A parent's heart, of sorrow to beguile,
Cheer an afflicted husband by a smile.
20 To bind the truant that's inclined to roam,
Good humour makes a paradise at home.
To raise the fallen, to pity and forgive,
This is our noblest, best prerogative.
By these, pursuing nature's gentle plan,
25 We hold in silken chains—the lordly tyrant man.

But pray, forgive this flippancy—indeed,
Of all your clemency I stand in need.
To own the truth, the scenes this night displayed,
Are only fictions—drawn by fancy's aid.
30 'Tis what I wish. But we have cause to fear,
No ray of comfort the sad bosoms cheer,
Of many a Christian, shut from light and day,
In bondage, languishing their lives away.

Say! You who feel humanity's soft glow,
35 What rapt'rous joy must the poor captive know;
Who, freed from slavery's ignominious chain,
Views his dear native land and friends again?

If there's a sense, more exquisitely fine,
A joy more elevated, more divine;
40 'Tis felt by those, whose liberal minds conceived,
The generous plan, by which he was relieved.

When first this glorious universe began,
And heaven to punish disobedient man
Sent to attend him, through life's dreary shade,
Affliction—poor dejected, weeping maid.   45
Then came Benevolence, by all revered,
He dried the mourner's tears, her heart he cheered;
He wooed her to his breast—made her his own,
And Gratitude appeared, their first-born son.
Since when, the father and the son has joined,   50
To shed their influence o'er the human mind:
And in the heart, where either deign to rest,
Rise transports, difficult to be expressed.
Such, as within your generous bosoms glow,
Who feel returned the blessings you bestow.   55
Oh! ever may you taste those joys divine,
While Gratitude—sweet Gratitude—is mine.

—1794